REPERCUSSIONS OF LOVE

A POETRY BOOK

BY

N.O.

TABLE OF CONTENTS

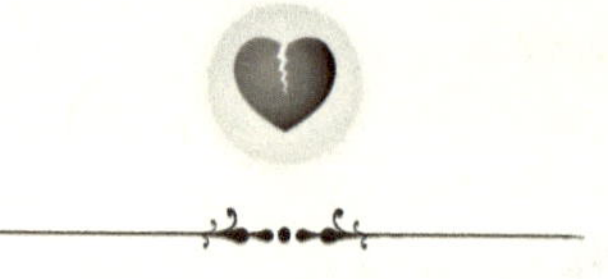

HELLO

Caught eyes, then you told me your name. Flirt a little as you brush up against me, I know the game. The physical attraction is undeniable, the energy between us warms the skin. For me, hearing your thoughts is where it begins. What are your loves, what breaks your heart? What would you change if you had a new start? What turns you on, makes you weak in the knees? Would you tell me your dreams if I say please? Where are you going, where have you been? What's important to me is that you let me in. How many times have you been hurt, have you a broken heart? See, I have to know the true you, before we can start. Do you let emotions get in the way when making a decision? Do you have time in your day and where could I fit in? Where's your favorite place, where would you love to go? Is your favorite music fast or slow? Do you like to dance, what makes your heart sing? Is your heart mending and will you let me in? Do you love to laugh, what do you find funny? Is it the simple things that are important or do you like money? What are your goals, how important are your ambitions? Who are your people, what are their traditions? Do you like your job or do you live for the weekends? Do you like a man that gives time or one who spends? Do you have children, if so, what are their names? Your last break up, is there still pain? Tell me a dream, are you living your truth? Do you like your man soft, is it alright that I can be a brute? When you think of your future, does it bring a smile? Are you looking for security or someone to drive you wild? Would you like to hold hands and stroll? Would you want me to take a backseat or should I take control? Have you been supported; have you been loved? Did he show you attention and was it enough? When he said I love you, did he show it as well? Have you said I love you before you fell? Are you willing to know me, give me a chance? If you're just looking for fun, sorry I don't do one-night stands.

LISTEN

You speak love without talking, can we be friends? It's like sex without moaning, if this isn't how it begins. Friendship is a must before we ever lay down. I have no time for you in life if your only interest is just to go to town. I must know you, what's in your heart. Without that it's failure before we start. I want to figure out how to make you smile, make sure we connect. Just trying to come correct. Treat you like a lady, someone to treasure. I want our souls to intertwine, then comes the pleasure.

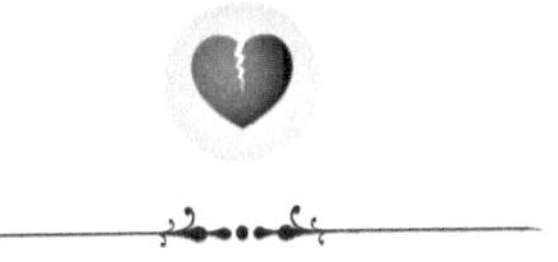

HESITANT HEARTS

Courageousness does come to mind
Two hearts wrapped in caution,
a futile resistance we've come to find

An inadequate shield defenseless
an once inaccessible realm,
now stricken relentless

Slight fractures allow love to slip within
rushing sensations swirl throughout,
inducing mind to spin

Love quickly falls helplessly from the lips
closeness retains the fire,
slowly taking turns while gently taking sips

Almost breathing for one another
sweet is the flavor
enlightened trust we use for cover,
in each other we savor.

DOUBT

Tell me your dreams, please let me know if I'm in them
Can I help them come true?
Are they dreams of us?
Or wishes for society
Now that's sexy
If your dreams come without conclusion
I'd say follow me, but I have no time for that
Live you, then live for others
Dream big
Dream for all
That's the hand I will hold
Love is only the first step

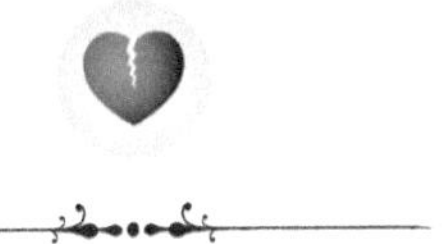

IRRESISTIBLE EYES

At times your eyes are all I can see
When I come to a blink, it's like an end to a dream
A dream from long ago
As I'm communicating with your soul
Or you may be seizing mine
If that's the case, that's just fine
The vibe you send, sets my soul at ease
One look from you is enough to calm this beast
The passion transcends, when you're near
Love can terrify, but with you I feel no fear
When lost in your eyes all my pain releases
Your glow seems able to connect all the pieces
A heart that I thought had gone black
Your spirit so brilliant, I can't react
I'm thankful for every touch
Every minute we embrace, our time is never too much

WARM EMBRACE

Wondering of wishing
Often laughing and dismissing
Longing for logic of circumstance
Waiting for a shaman's trance
Dreams of life unobserved
Ode to a mind undisturbed
Only love seems to matter
The passion when lovers gather
Harnessed by what should be
A life of freedom is all I see
All of life is love
Energy seeps from above

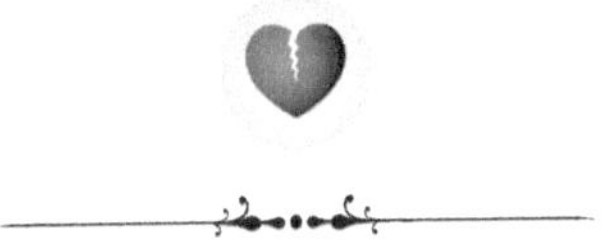

SOFT TOUCH

Kisses slowly and softly down her spine
An angel in the flesh, a taste of the divine

No time to rush
Every second a treasure
Like a painter's brush
Creating strokes of pleasure

Feeling her electric soul
Energy abundance
Knowledge of a transcendent role
As mystical as the sun dance

An awakened dream
Hearts beat as one
An endless stream
Two rivers combining to run

Kisses...
Slowly...
Softly...
Down...
Her...
Spine...

EVERY DROP

Your soft, sweet voice
These strong hands
Wet
I pull you close
Your chest upon mine
Wet
Embracing your soft skin
Friction in time
Wet
You take control
Unleash your soul
Wet
You, washing my sins
While I become yours

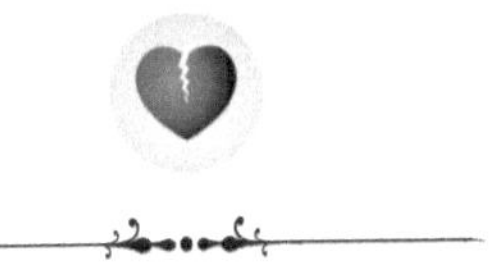

IMMEASURABLE BEAUTY

Ease on the eyes doesn't even scratch the surface
Although the numbing vision almost blinds
Look beyond to see the truth
That is where love is found
And that is where sorrow is drowned
Not in a bottle, but rather a drink from the lips
Selling my soul seems to narrowly cover the bill
It's only natural to ask why
Knowing that is an answer I do not crave
It can make you stand tall
Yet bring you to your knees to beg for forgiveness
Then lift you up with a single word
Just a glance can stir you with craze
Yet, with just one touch can keep you sane
To lose can feel like death
Knowing for just one moment, is worth my last breath

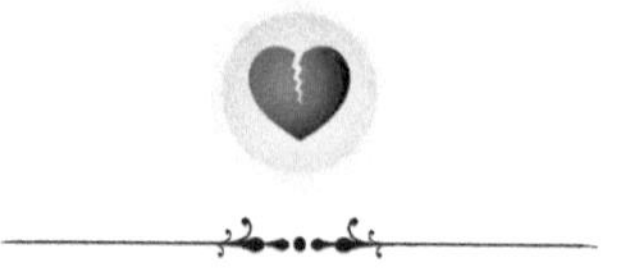

ENTICEMENT

Collarbone, dark hair and deep brown eyes
High cheek bones, slender waist and soft smooth thighs
Long legs, kissable neck and luscious lips
Pretty toes, angelic complexion and a will mesmerize
with a shake of the hips
Hands that I must hold, a back that begs to be caressed
Shoulders to massage and an ass that is truly blessed
Breasts that are only surpassed by what is beneath
Your beating heart sings me to sleep
My eyes beg to comprehend the enigmatic vision that
is you
Beauty that is true

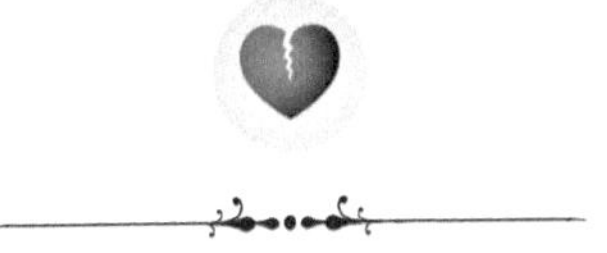

WHY

Why can't she love me in the way that'll let her
Kind
So brilliant in her gentleness
Beautiful
A refined sense of truth
If only
I could never see myself as she does

HEAVEN

Closely held
Softly spoken
Wrapped around
Wisdom being whispered
I have no reply
The sense of being cherished
A sweet kiss on my cheek
Feeling a heartbeat
Only the sound is sweet
Dreams while awakened, surely divine
Lust
Love
Resilience lost
Take what I am given
What else is there

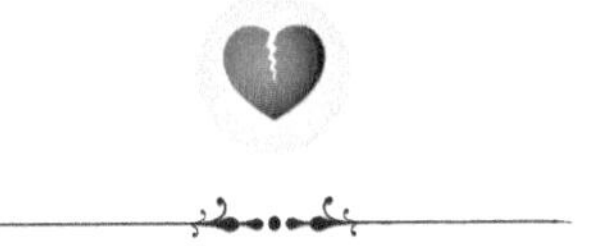

DEAR PATIENCE

Kind
Absolving spirit
Gentle touch, loving gaze
No matter how far I went
I always came home
With hate
I was matched with love
I pushed away
You held tight
You finally released
I'll spend eternity wanting

FRIENDS

We laugh
Then laugh some more
Touches
Ever so slight
Laugh, laugh, laugh
Embrace
Laugh
Hold, wishing to never let go
Gentle hands upon each other's faces
A halfhearted laugh leads to a kiss
Soft passion
Dreams of what could not be
One night that was
Wrong place and time
Forbidden happiness
What could have been
We will never know

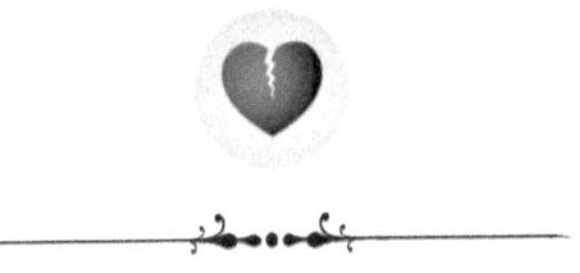

ANGEL

For so long, she tried to drag me to God
Pure in soul
I was so far away
She would lift me up
mostly with compassion
I would drag her back down
with hours of passion
Lust always won

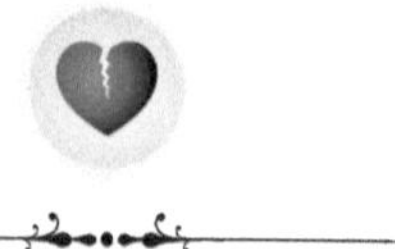

UNFORGIVING FRACTURE

How did you ever shine through?
Abuse as a child
Death of one
Unnoticed by the other
A snaked slipped in
A pain unimaginable for most
With a chance to heal, I failed
Still your smile brightens the world that treated you so
unkind
Yet, that smile brings pain for the love I could not bring
Cruelty in the end is all I feel I added
Understanding is what you deserved
My one regret
We met
when I was not yet a man

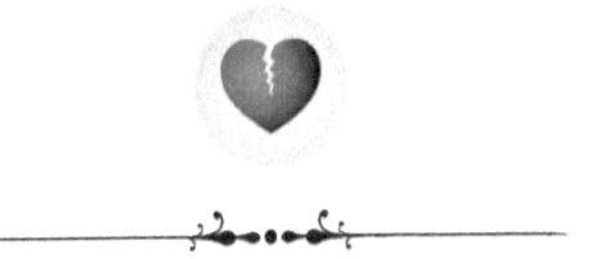

EARTHQUAKE

Lust drips from the lips
Eyes pierce the soul
Bite on the neck
Nails in my back
Embrace
Release
Teasing has become second nature
Blood racing
Try to keep up
Wall
Floor
Indoors, outdoors
Front and back
Top and bottom
Breathe
Just breathe

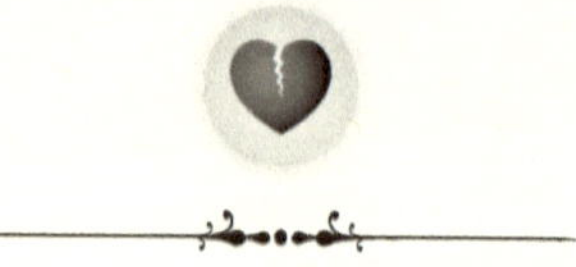

DARKNESS STANDS

Dark eyes
Dark thighs
Mesmerize
No clear thoughts
Careless in being lost
Sexy is boss
One vision is hers
Melt on the curves
There truly are no words
My arms wrapped around
her soft voice, a tender sound
An infatuation is what I've found
If I could only last
savoring the memories even before time has passed

SEE YOUR TRUTH

Beauty I see with such ease
I saw with just a glance
Yet, you have the mirror
How can you not
break thru the fog of society
forget what the unworthy have taught
Superficial sickness should be shoved to the side
Those with less, often try to blind one to their self
See what I see
Truly look
Then never blink

PASSION

The passion in my heart is her
In her eyes, you see the craze stir
She loves so hard, it may seem like hate
Her rage spills over, on to her mate
She can hurt what she loves

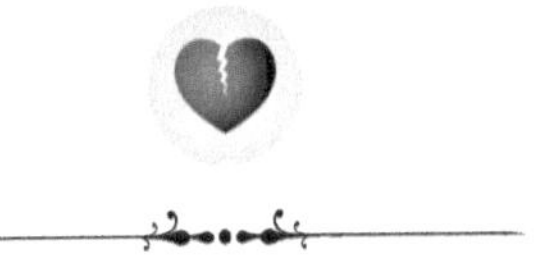

MY WEAKNESS

I went in so deep,
I touched her heart
I didn't know the chaos,
That I would start
Tears in her eyes,
With love on her lips
No matter how hard I tried,
I could never call it quits
Hearts pounding and racing,
Whenever near
Cupid lost his arrows,
This time used a spear
The bleeding won't stop,
No matter how hard I try
I beg and plead with my heart, yet
I get no reply
Begging and breaking
Down to my knees
I always give in
My love will never cease
Finally, I relinquish my fight for all time
My strength, my weakness, mine

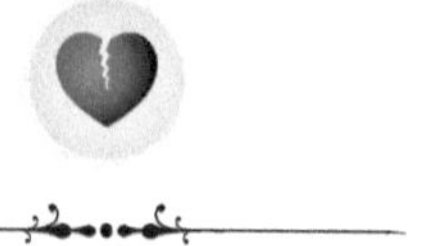

THE GAMES WE PLAY

Youth is crazy and spontaneous in its thoughts of reality
Maturity will never catch up, no matter how wise it can
be
Lust for fun, laughing death in the face
Mild amusement with death's embrace
When it slows for love, tragedy slides down
All souls get crazy when lust is around
Fuck all the noise, she can't handle the touch
When this man comes to play, it's always too much

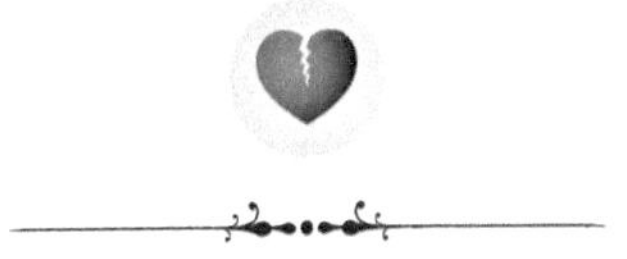

AGONIZING

My passive mind screams to bring some tranquility upon my fervent heart. Yet when it is love, patience will often vanish swiftly. A catastrophe is rarely unforeseen in matters of love, rather merely ignored. The lure of that one, brings with it an insanity of the soul. Lustful intense desire clenches ahold of logic, making it sound harsh and unwanted. My haven of her in embrace, elusive as it may be at times, brings peace to a spirit ripe with anguish. Agitation has never been more welcomed by someone so full of doubt, diving towards a life of pure distraction. Optimism is only an amusement yet is treasured by she who dares comprehend the bear that is me.

LOST LOVE

My mouth dissolves when I try to speak
The thoughts you give
I wish we could talk
Walk away
There is just know comprehension
All my messages
Must be hell to be so shut down
Was it me?
A futile question I guess at
In a bed is where all our agreements came
Change of life strikes me
With wings clipped, I can't fly
All I can do is say goodbye

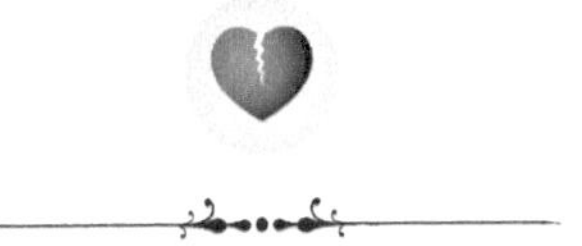

RATIONALIZING LOVE

Feminine brilliance is where the idea of god presides
It is but a dream to reside in her presence
Masculinity is a joke in comparison
Wake up
Soft spoken words tend to hide the domination
Dreams of power are just a myth
Hold her tight
Hang on to brilliance
The work is not letting go

RAVEN

Deep raven hair, smooth brown skin, deep dark eyes
and a devious bright smile.
Even though I know better, I dig your style. Funny how
the mind is so easily
Deceived when the eyes are entranced by what they
see. Knowing deep in my
Soul the vision is merely a dream wrapped around
a nightmare.

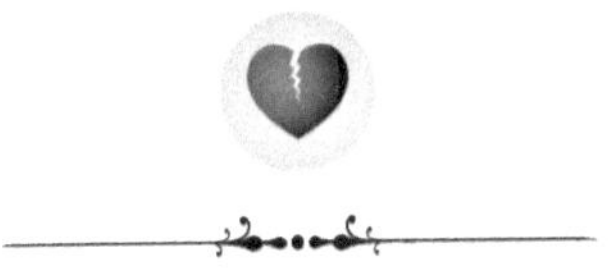

SAD

The sad clown or an act
I can't even tell
What's false, what's fact

But I stay true to myself
You still haven't even looked in the mirror
Can't even recognize that you fell

Standing tall in your own mind
Truly you're still crawling
Maybe if you opened your eyes, you could see the signs

Always stepping on toes
You spent half your life chasing
Then get hurt when people let out those words, sluts
and hoes

It's easy to see you don't love yourself
Damn, give yourself a hug
There's no time to cry about the cards that were dealt

You're stuck in delusions
Please don't give into tragedy

I'M SORRY, YOU'RE STILL SORRY

I hate you is all I say
It hurts, even though I know that it's just one more lie
You miss my love
You miss my touch
Life ain't the same
Just what you tell yourself to dull the pain
You miss my big heart, amongst other thangs
You cry and cry
Wishing I was still drying your tears
Now you 're stuck feeling alone with another sharing your bed
Gotta move on
Gotta move on
That's the problem in not loving yourself
You have to depend on others
Dependence is a pain that can last a lifetime.

IDIVIUALISTIC FEROCITY

Why can't this women fess up
Sorry, love, I don't mean to interrupt
Your little tantrum
But you look offended just because I want some
It wasn't long ago that you couldn't get enough
We both know that you're a freak and like it rough
Now there's no sweat then relaxation
Knowing what you have is a fixation
You chased so long
You couldn't see I was wrong
Now you can't handle what you have
So, pout and act sad
I need someone true
That someone, isn't you
You say you dig my passion
When you fly high, there will always be some crashing
So, when you leave, I won't sigh
There will be another passing by

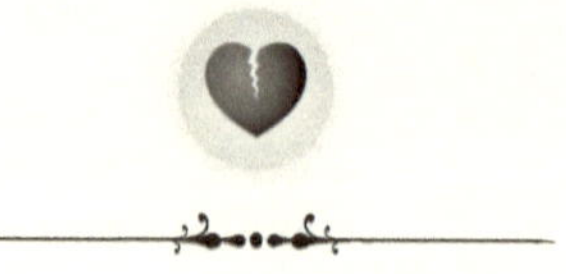

ENFEEBLED LOVE

The inharmonious sound of her voice
fractures my spirit
I hate you
is how I hear it
All I can say
It's not you it's me
Then wander on
Let her think she's won
Does it matter
like it's a prize
when the other one's sadder
Crazed with low self esteem
Oh, I'm always so mean
I guess it must hurt not to like what you see in the mirror
That makes you shallow or that's how it appears
Goodbye miss
Lucky for you, ignorance is bliss

LUCKY ME

Lucky me
Down on my bloody knees
Passion often overcomes pain
Internal, external makes no difference
My first taste of divinity
Left begging for more
Pleasing the goddess

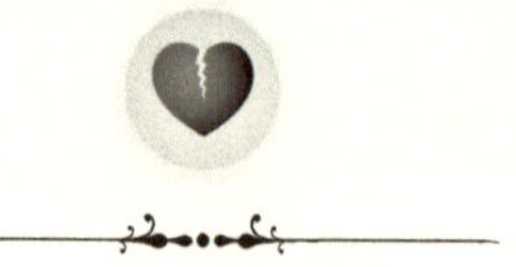

I CAN'T FIND MY WAY

She gives me direction
I shake it off
Offering salvation
I say fuck off

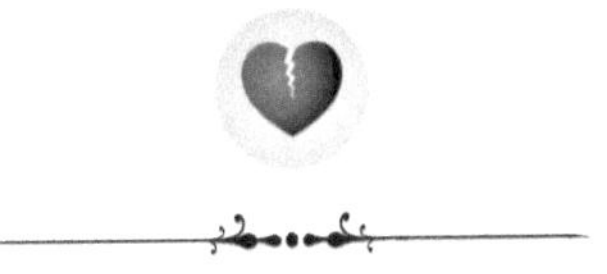

MY FIRST LOVE

I try to find her in every woman
I keep looking
Looking
Looking
She's not there

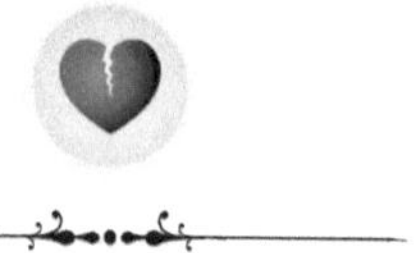

PUSH AND PULL

Pull me close
I grab ahold tightly
Pull me close, no resistance
She deserves more, shoots through my mind
She's not looking for love, at least as it is defined
She's just lost
Forgotten her worth
I try to remind
Sing praises of gold
Pull me close
Time is good
Relax, refine
She wants only passion
So, I give her distraction

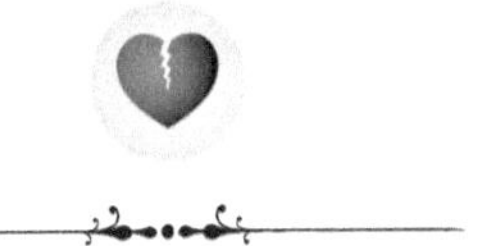

CRASH

Grasping
Grabbing a hold of want
Take me as I am
Foolish thought
Try to change me if you will
A creator you are not
You may control me in your thighs
Once released, relative disappointment drops from your eyes
Grasp, detain if you want
Smoke through fingers
You hold nothing in the end

SO

Lustful temptation
Both hands slip
Try
Grab ahold
Impossible
Unwavering freedom
Give up
Sparing oneself, is an often overlooked part of love

WASTED TIME

Let me be, I cry
Holding so tight
I have what you don't need
Tighter you squeeze
Can't breathe
Shake loose of your dreams
Believe your fears
I'm always out of your reach

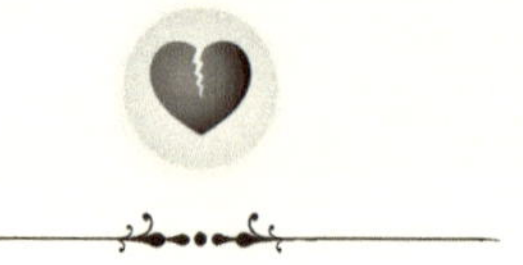

THOUGHT I WAS CLOSE

Some days, there was love
Darkness always returned
Willing to fight to the death
Sadness always conquered
Why?
My love was powerless
Inept
My begging ignored
By God and by her
This painful realization made me spit fire
Cursing the creator along with her insanity
Then dropping down, as obedient as I could be
To love that which can not reciprocate
A hell known, but not feared
Hate is truly closest to true love
A passion which shall always stay unconquered
I look to the sky in disgust
Hell above
Left to forever mistrust

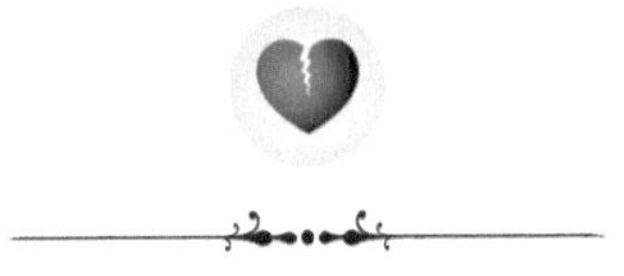

QUIVER

First time for everything
Chill in the air tonight
Exposed in the open
Steam rises from our bodies and the water
Alone, but could be seen at any moment
Fear often intensifies pleasure
Adrenaline, the most overlooked drug
Nerves thrown beyond intrigue
Over in minutes
Yet, lasts forever

RELEASED SPIRIT

Forgetting the past by remembering the future
Memories of love couldn't be fewer
Pains of mistrust
Bury what was once untamed lust
A wilderness of emotions
Knowledge of contention erases all devotion
Inhospitable space surrounds her
Faithfulness is far from her nature
She has no honor
She has no plea
She has no love
She has no me

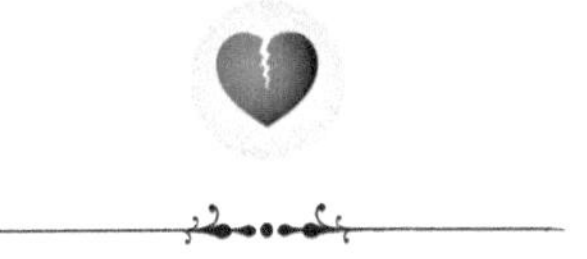

MEMORIES

Is it strange that I can still taste your lips
Feel your warmth
The heat of your kiss

When you 're in view I can't help but stare
I lay awake at night
from the smell of your hair

I am cursed with memories, finding no rest
Your hug around my neck
When it came to us, it was never just sex

Always left longing for more touch
Going crazy
I try to understand how memories of pleasure can hurt
so much

I can't remember most of the year
I can't help but remember
Our first time and wiping away your tears

From your heartbreaking cry
To the joy in your laugh
Now our final goodbye

SPARK

I lost my words when you first said hi. A touch from your hand brought me back to life. Sparks flew when I caught the slightest glance of the sparkle in your eye. That fuzzy feeling brought cotton to my mouth. Any silk smooth talk fell back into my spine. Sweet tones gently slid into my ears. Treating me so kind. Never have I heard pure love glide off a tongue.

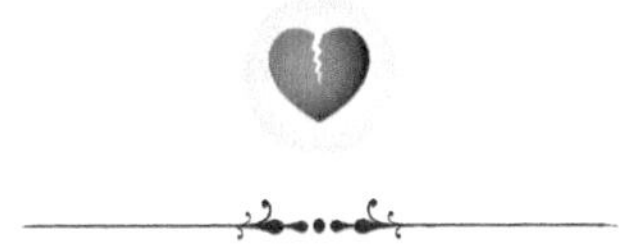

GENTLE SOUL

Gentle ways
Softens my heart
You bring such curiosity
A sense of one
Soft
Soft spoken
Hard
Hard woken
Taken by the hand, guided by my heart
I once dreamed I was enough
Now I'm in the sad state of believing
Carried by vibes
Mostly my own
Haunted by the wisdom of loss
Still, I feel a little peace

AWAKE

With life starts pain,
In distress begins conversion,
Modifications are not always sane.
Empathy for one's self brings notions of despair,
Yet sympathy lets us purge through our care.

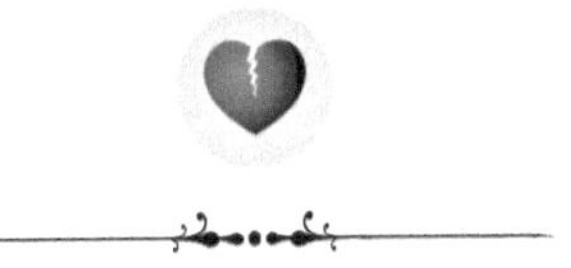

HEALER

My healer, my teacher, my lover, my friend
Though I'm unworthy I try to pretend
Always lost in your eyes
Try to hide my darkness
So as not to dim the light that is you
Knowing I could never forgive myself
To cause a single tear
Would break my spirit
Recovery hopeless

THE END